十二月的节日

Customs, Traditions and Landmarks |
Non-Fiction Series

Copyright © 2022 by Level Learning, INC. and Washington Yu Ying PCS™
Original and Edited Text Copyright © 2022 by Washington Yu Ying PCS™

All rights reserved. No part of this book in whole or part may be reproduced without written permission from the publisher.

Published by Level Learning, INC.

Content Contributors:
Washington Yu Ying PCS™
Level Learning - Ya-Ching Chang

Illustrations by: Josh Taira

Leveling classification based on Level Learning standard. For full description, visit www.levellearning.com

ISBN 978-1-64040-011-5
Simplified Chinese Edition

About Level Learning:
Level Learning provides a literacy focused curriculum specifically designed for K-12 Chinese as a Second Language classrooms. Our program offers 20 levels of specific and detailed objectives, leveled texts and passages, mastery-based online assessment, and analytics to enable data-driven instruction. Level Learning reading curriculum for both literature and informational text emphasize grammar and comprehension skills to help teachers develop confident and independent Chinese language readers. The non-fiction series of books are specifically designed to support our informational text course based on multiple national standards. To learn more about our entire offering, visit www.levellearning.com

About Washington Yu Ying PCS™:
Washington Yu Ying PCS is a Mandarin English dual language immersion International Baccalaureate (IB) World school. Yu Ying's mission is to inspire and prepare young people to create a better world by challenging them to reach their full potential in a nurturing Chinese/English educational environment. Yu Ying's comprehensive IB, dual immersion curriculum equips students with global competencies for success in the real world. As a leader in immersion education, Yu Ying is determined to advance Chinese language programs and global citizenry education by helping other schools create and strengthen their Chinese programs. For more information, email: products@washingtonyuying.org

十二月						
星期一	星期二	星期三	星期四	星期五	星期六	星期日
	1	2	3	4	5	6
7	8	9	10	11	12	13
14	15	16	17	18	19	20
21	22	23	24	25	26	27
28	29	30	31			

在十二月，美国有哪些节日呢？有圣诞节，还有光明节和宽扎节。

光明节是犹太人的节日。人们通常会庆祝八天八夜。

庆祝的时候，人们会点蜡烛。每天点一根，一共八根。

这些蜡烛会被放在窗户旁边。

在光明节,人们会玩陀螺游戏。人们还会吃油炸面团。

	十二月						
星期一	星期二	星期三	星期四	星期五	星期六	星期日
	1	2	3	4	5	6
7	8	9	10	11	12	13
14	15	16	17	18	19	20
21	22	23	24	25	26	27
28	29	30	31	一月 1		

宽扎节是非洲裔美国人的节日。人们通常会庆祝七天七夜。

庆祝的时候,人们会点蜡烛。每天点一根,一共七根。

家里的装饰品,有红色的,有绿色的,还有黑色的。

人们会唱歌和讲故事。

人们还会吃非洲食物。

Glossary

	Pinyin	English Definition
节日	jié rì	festival
圣诞节	shèng dàn jié	Christmas
光明节	guāng míng jié	Hanukkah
宽扎节	kuān zhā jié	Kwanzaa
犹太人	yóu tài rén	Jewish people
庆祝	qìng zhù	to celebrate
蜡烛	là zhú	candle
窗户	chuāng hù	window
旁边	páng biān	next to
陀螺	tuó luó	dreidel
油炸面团	yóu zhá miàn tuán	fried doughnut
非洲裔	fēi zhōu yì	African descent
装饰品	zhuāng shì pǐn	decoration

www.ingramcontent.com/pod-product-compliance
Lightning Source LLC
Chambersburg PA
CBHW041222070526
44584CB00001B/56